I Was Born a Winner

I Was Born a Winner

By

Claston A. Bernard

A journey from a life of discouragement on the rocky playgrounds to the Olympic Games, a Commonwealth gold medal, and fulfillment.

© 2018 Claston A. Bernard
All rights reserved.

ISBN: 1985425815
ISBN 13: 978-1985425811
Library of Congress Control Number: 2018902142

CreateSpace Independent Publishing Platform
North Charleston, South Carolina

To Quantez, my beautiful wife, and my beautiful family. Thank you for allowing me the time to put my thoughts together. To my parents, Claston E. and Florence Bernard thanks for your sacrifices. I love you guys. Sisters, Andrea and Toya and brother Preston, much love. Andrea, you are the best big sister a brother could ask for.

To all the friends and coaches that supported me, nuff love!

Table of Contents

Page

Preface 7

Chapter One – How It All Started 11

Chapter Two – Munro College 31

Chapter Three – A New Journey 41

Chapter Four – A New Purpose 54

Chapter Five – The Decathlon 68

Chapter Six – Louisiana State University 76

Chapter Seven – Life as a Pro 98

Chapter Eight – The Picture Becomes Clearer 122

Preface

I grew up in Jamaica in the district of Burnt Savannah, St. Elizabeth, between Lacovia and Mountainside. That's about a twenty-minute drive from Santa Cruz, St. Elizabeth. Life was tough for me as a child. While we lived in poverty, my parents did the best they could for my siblings and me. I was often called names and ridiculed—by some adults as well as kids. I was considered awkward and was an easy target because I was a quiet kid and kept to myself. That behavior even led some people to think I was an idiot.

I loved to read and explore the hills near my home. Some people saw my passion for reading and tried to discourage it, but more than anything I wanted to go to university. Discouragement was a constant for me. Everyone had an opinion about my life even though I wasn't sharing my dreams with them or asking for their opinions. I wanted out of poverty and, more importantly, I wanted to leave all the discouragement behind. I knew I needed to go to university, but how?

Little did I realize that the early discouragements I faced in my community were preparing me for what was to come on my journey in high school and life in general. This story is about that journey and the different roads, venues, and vehicles I took to reach my goals, and the hand that guided me.

Despite the challenges of growing up materially poor, a good investment in education and sacrifices by my parents gave me the opportunity to attend one of Jamaica's best high schools, Munro College. Attending Munro was the catalyst that led a local boy to make history by becoming a Jamaican international gold medalist, a two-time Olympian, an American NCAA champion, and one of the top decathletes in the world.

Join me as I journey from the rocky playgrounds of Burnt Savannah to Boys Champs, the CARIFTA Games, the

NCAA track and field championships, the Olympic Games, and a Commonwealth Games gold medal. What was most telling on my journey was that there was always a force working against me. But as the words of the popular 2015 reggae song "My Dream" by Nesbeth say, "Look at me now, weh them treat mi less than good, put me inna box like a rectangle." I was put in a box by many, but how would I break out?

In the end, there was the finger of the Master Painter whom I later came to understand more clearly was guiding my every step. I was welcomed back to my hometown of Burnt Savannah as a hero and an icon and, most importantly, I learned how powerful it is to forgive. It was great to see my community celebrating one of their own and having something to make them happy.

This story will give specific dates, times, and details about major athletic events in which I competed. It starts with me in basic school (pre-K), then primary school, high school, and university. It will describe my earliest competitions from a cricket pitch to Olympic stadiums. My experiences traveling the world will tell how I finally realized that true happiness is not all about winning or accomplishing your goals. In pursuing athletic supremacy, I came to realize that it did not provide the satisfaction I had envisioned. That fact occurred to me while traveling to two major cities on my way to the 2004 Olympic Games. That's when I realized that athletic fame only left me wanting and empty.

Chapter One

How It All Started

It was 1983, and I was four years old. It was Sports Day at Burnt Savannah Basic School sports playground, which was about a quarter mile trek from the school compound itself. Some parts of the field were rocky and sloped toward the southern end. There were wooden football (soccer) goalposts on the field that ran north to south. In the middle of the playground was a cricket pitch about sixty yards (20.15) meters long by nine yards (3 meters) wide.

The middle of the pitch was where the race would be run. Parents surrounded the pitch while students raced. I remember being prodded from behind when it was my time to run. A girl whose name I do not remember came running to me, and I took off . . .

In 1986 I was seven years old, and it was Sports Day again, but this time at Burnt Savannah Primary School. I was running the 100 meters with a blue bandana wrapped around my head. It was blue for the house I represented at school that was named after George William Gordon, one of Jamaica's national heroes. The playground ran east to west with wooden goalposts that were surrounded by barbed wire fences to the south and east and wire fences that faced west toward the street. The lanes of the track were lined with marl (lime), and the northern side of the field was mostly rocky. I don't remember if I won the race that day, but the worst case scenario would have been second place because the only kid in my age group who could have beaten me was Omar Robinson, affectionately called Gabbie.

But I do remember crossing the halfway mark in that 100-meter race and hearing a reggae song playing over the sound system. It was Freddie McGregor, a famous reggae artist since the late 1970s who had been born in 1956 in the parish of Clarendon. I fell in love with Freddie's music at that moment and found myself running to the beat of the song.

In 1992 Freddie released "I Was Born a Winner," which I adopted as my theme song throughout the rest of my life as an athlete. That song helped me reflect on what it meant to be a winner because I had never fully grasped the concept.

* * *

I was born at home in 1979 in the district of Burnt Savannah in the parish of St. Elizabeth in southwest Jamaica. My home was sandwiched between two churches, the Burnt Savannah Baptist Church, which was separated only by a fence from the Brethren Church and by my granduncle's house. Burnt Savannah is located between Locovia to the north and Mountain Side to the south with the Santa Cruz Mountains to the east and the Black River Swamp to the west. My Parents were Claston E. (Longman/Longas) Bernard and Florence (Fernie) Bernard. My father was a mason by trade and a farmer. My mother ran things at home like Napoleon. They were the best parents a child could have, especially growing up in our environment.

We lived in a two-bedroom house with detached kitchen and latrine with my three siblings Andrea, the oldest; Preston (Pres); and Amoy (Toya), the baby. We had no electricity or running water; we couldn't afford them. We used kerosene to light lamps at night and to run our stove, but only on special occasions. Most of the cooking was done over wood in the outside kitchen.

For as long as I can remember I loved to read, and I had an active imagination. My parents made education a priority for us because they saw it as our path out of poverty. My memory is fuzzy on this, but I remember reading about an unfortunate boy named Dick Whittington and his cat. Dick lived in England, but he was about to journey off to seek his fortune when he heard the chime of a clock that he thought was telling him to turn back. After reading that story I often wondered what it would be like to travel the world. I would see the planes high in the sky and wonder where they were going and what adventures awaited the passengers.

My life was full of questions from an early age, and living close to churches made it impossible not to have many about religion. Who is God? What is my purpose? I always felt there was a hand guiding my every move, but whose hand was it?

I was a daydreamer who lived inside my head and my books. But my daydreaming often would be cut short by my mother loudly calling me to do some chores.

My early childhood was structured around school, church, chores, and more chores. From age five it was my responsibility to wash dishes, rake the yard with coconut branches, fetch firewood, fill the drums and drinking buckets with water, water the cows and goats and, along with my older brother Preston, feed the pigs. And when all that was done, there were usually plenty of other odd jobs that needed done around our home.

To get water we would travel about a quarter mile daily to the standpipe that served our community. On Saturday, washing day, we could make as many as twenty trips to fetch water for washing the clothes. We carried five-gallon buckets on our heads, and sometimes we carried one on our head and one in our hand to reduce the number of trips. My mom diligently carried out the washing of our clothes—all by hand—including my father's cement-filled garments. Her hands often were covered with blisters from all that washing.

After fetching water I would accompany Preston to fetch firewood for the week. That task could be a three-mile trip into the swamp or mountains. The wood we preferred for firewood was logwood. The logwood tree's botanical name is haematoxylum campechianum. "Haematoxylum" means bloodwood. The tree is a legume. The little green pods are edible and are native to southern Mexico and parts of Central America. The tree, noted for its pretty yellow blossoms and pleasant scent, was used to make fence posts and, when dried, was used for cooking. It tended to burn a long time and gave the food a wonderful flavor. It was brought to Jamaica by the English who used to raid Spanish territories. The English used the wood to make dye that would turn purple when hot and brownish when it cooled. Once when I was fetching firewood and was a few miles from home I was stung by a scorpion lodged in the bundle of wood. I almost fainted, but I was determined to carry the wood home because daily meals depended on the availability of wood.

Another moment that has stuck in my head from my early childhood involved staying up late and listening to the crickets with my older brother into the wee hours of the mornings. Then we would wake up early on little sleep and accompany our dad as he moved the cows around the pasture. I did not have to do that, but waking up early with my dad was something I looked forward to. I enjoyed feeling the dew between my toes as we trekked to the hills to find the cows while it was still dark. Those were special moments because I was able to spend time with my dad before he headed off to work.

Nothing much was said along the trek, but just having him beside me was deeply reassuring. My dad was a determined, hard-working man who provided for us and, if I didn't catch him in the mornings before work, by the time he got home he was tired, and it was time for me to be in bed.

I remember watching my dad farming peanuts on a two-acre strip of land, and when everyone else would take a break, he would keep on working, only stopping to take a sip of water despite being bent over from sunrise to sunset. Dad's work ethic had a great impact on me. He showed me what it meant to be disciplined and to stay with a task until the end.

It would be hard to believe now, but as a child I was seriously quiet. I enjoyed reading more than anything, and when I woke up in the morning my nose often would be black from the soot of the kerosene lamp after having read for hours. I remember that lamp shade read, "Home Sweet Home."

Whenever I was out in public I would say little to anyone beyond greeting them. I preferred keeping to myself. I lived in my head, and that gave the wrong impression to many people who thought my silence meant I was an idiot. That was a tough stigma for a child to carry. But then matters got worse.

At my graduation from basic school we were presented with our certificates. As each child's name was called by the presenter he would offer congratulations, and the child would respond with a thank you. But I was so excited and caught up in getting an opportunity to speak into a microphone for the first time that when it was my turn to say thank you, instead I said—as loud as I could—"Congratulations!" It would have been a funny moment, but I was laughed at hysterically by almost everyone. Frequently afterward I was reminded of that moment, and it was used by many as proof of how stupid I was. That insulting behavior not only came from young kids but adults as well. I would be sent to the shop to purchase food, and I would hear the adults talking about how I was an idiot. They didn't even try to be discreet about it; they acted as if I wasn't there. But years later I came to appreciate the word "congratulations" on many prominent occasions.

* * *

Going to church was an integral part of our family life. We attended the Burnt Savannah Baptist Church—Sunday School first and then the church service. It may be difficult to imagine, but despite living between two churches separated only by a fence, we still managed to be late from time to time, or we would miss Sunday worship altogether. When we did attend church it was fascinating to hear the praise and worship; it was almost mystical as the building itself seemed to come alive.

As much as I enjoyed church, I also loved the game of cricket. I couldn't get enough. I would go to the playground on Sundays to watch cricket after church. If I could've gotten away with it, I would have missed church altogether to see those games. I enjoyed playing the game too; I would play with some boys from my community with bats made from coconut branches and wickets made from whatever sticks we could find and a tennis ball or even a golf ball. Even at school I could not wait for recess so I could play cricket with my friends. I also enjoyed soccer, but because soccer balls were so hard to come by we would play with juice boxes, so the interest in soccer was not as high. After all, juice boxes just don't roll like a soccer ball.

Growing up in a materially poor country does not mean that the land is not rich and bountiful. In fact, I would consider Jamaica an oasis, a country rich in everything you can imagine growing on the land. It was hard to go hungry in rural Jamaica. No matter how little food we had at home, if I was hungry enough during the day, I could climb a tree anywhere and find food to fill my belly.

It was a sight watching the sun rising over the mountains early in the mornings from the front of our home, and I soaked up the beauty. Other times, watching it rain on the Santa Cruz Mountains was grandeur itself, and seeing the rainbow after the rain gave you much to ponder about one of life's greatest symbols. What hand created such a wonder?

There were times my imagination would take me wandering into the mountains to hunt birds and search for fruit. I loved the hills. There I found peace and tranquility where I could escape into my make-believe world. From the hills I could see my home and the swamps far in the background. It is an amazing thing to see the glory of the created world from a higher vantage point. Looking from one direction at a picture doesn't always reveal its true beauty or what the creator intended, especially when you're part of the picture. Sometimes the creator wants you to look the other way to truly appreciate his handy work. Those moments made climbing the hills a worthwhile excursion. Instead of viewing the hills from the bottom up, I saw them from the top down.

Burnt Savannah

In the district of Burnt Savannah there were only a few people who encouraged me, and those who did were mostly the elderly. Looking back now, I can say it may not have been a bad thing. I guess those older folks saw something in me that I had not yet seen in myself. But that was not the case with some of the younger generation.

I was teased constantly about my demeanor, about the size of our home, about how my parents raised us to respect rules.

What I did not fully understand at the time was that my parents were investing in our futures rather than their own. That's why we didn't enjoy the same luxury as some of those around us. Most people seemed more interested in owning a bigger house and a fancier car. When I would be seen carrying books home from school, which I did often, I was told that books and studying too much made people go crazy. I guess they said that to keep me from aspiring for a better life.

I remember one instance when I was playing soccer with a group of guys and I made a good move, but it was not well received by many on the field because it had been performed by someone who was "crazy" and, therefore, by someone who should not be able to make such a move. The whole group of boys turned on me and called me names until it became a rock-throwing contest. I eventually ran to the safety of my home.

Schooling

The Burnt Savannah Basic School sat on top of Baptist Hill. The compound of the Burnt Savannah Baptist Church was where I attended basic school from age two to six. I started school earlier than most. My parents could not keep me from going because the school was directly in front of our home. The principal was the no-nonsense Mrs. Banton. At basic school we were prepared for primary school, which started at age six. Basic school was not a daycare; we wore uniforms and were taught to read and write. My days were spent building friendships, chasing butterflies, climbing fruit trees with friends, and climbing under the crawlspace looking for pencils and money that other students might have dropped through the floorboards. I used that found money to buy buns and cheese and suck-suck (frozen Kool-Aid).

I attended primary school from 1985 until 1991. The school was located about a mile from home, and we had to walk, rain or shine. We ran all the way if we were in danger of being late. Getting to school late was not in our best interest because you would be lined up in the principal's office to be disciplined.

The students were grouped based on our learning abilities. You were either in group A, group B, or the remedial class for those with learning disabilities. You could move from one group to another if your performance improved or declined. My early years at primary school brought me in contact with many students from other districts. They did not see me the way most people from my community did. My silence and adventurous ways were not viewed as odd. That fact made me want to be at school all the time. Furthermore, because I was a hard worker, I was given many responsibilities, and in grade six I was nominated to be deputy head boy by students, teachers, and our principal, Mr.

Stanley Walker, whom I believe to be one of the greatest principals and educators Jamaica has ever produced. I started seeing the world differently. I excelled in primary school, especially in spelling and athletics. I was not a nerd by any means, but I loved to read, and most of my recess was spent storytelling with friends or playing cricket, soccer, karate, or run down and catch. I had great friends in primary school. Dave Ellis is still one of the best storytellers and artists I have ever met, and Gary Edwards, Omar Robinson, Enroy Dunkley (my cousin) and, later, Ronald "Pops" Pendergrass also make my list of best childhood friends.

Principal Walker had transformed Burnt Savannah Primary into one of the top primary schools in Jamaica, and under his guidance it produced many parish spelling bee champions, my eldest sister Andrea Bernard being the first. Principal Walker was one of the few who believed in me more than I realized at the time.

One day while grade five spelling bee tryouts were going on I was outside playing cricket with my friends. Principal Walker called me in to join the spelling bee tryouts against the school heavyweights. Some of the guys I went up against that day are now lawyers, architects, and engineers. I had nothing to lose, and you did not turn Mr. Walker down when he asked you to take part in something. I ended up winning the boys' competition and represented our school along with the eventual parish champion, Ms. Synovia Cranston.

In grade six you had to take the Common Entrance Exam—I think now it's called the GSAT—to determine which school you would go to after primary. You did not go to school based on where you lived; you had to earn your placement. You could end up at a secondary school where you learned mainly crafts, at a technical school where academics and crafts split the focus, or high school where the higher-performing academic students tended to go. In my world, the school I would end up in didn't matter. I didn't fully comprehend the impact the different schools could have on my life, and that unawareness may have saved me plenty of trouble and stress. I didn't feel the pressure that I see students endure now as they compete for admission to Jamaica's top high schools. In fact, before you took the Common Entrance Exam you were supposed to list three choices of schools, but I didn't list any, so Mr. Walker chose for me. Thank God he did.

Sometime about May of 1991 I remember playing box ball with the girls at school. Box ball was played with a tennis ball or a juice box, and you would hit the ball or box as far as you could. Then you would run to your base, kind of like baseball. We had finished taking the Common Entrance Exam and were getting ready to graduate primary school when, in the midst of playing box ball, I saw my baby sister Toya and Neil, my best friend Gary's brother, racing toward us with a loud commotion trailing them. They were shouting, "You passed! You passed! You passed for Munro!"

"What is Munro?" I asked myself. But caught up in the jubilation, I ran a mile home to tell my mother. My dad was working in Canada at the time and would not return until fall. He used to travel to Canada for a farm work program for up to six months at a time to help supplement the family income so he could afford to put my siblings and me through school.

Chapter Two

Munro College

In Arce Sitam Quis Occultabit – Munro College Motto

Munro's motto translates to "A city set upon a hill cannot be hidden," and it remains true. Munro College High School, formerly Potsdam, is still a prominent boarding school for boys in St Elizabeth, Jamaica. It was founded in 1856 as a free school for poor boys in St. Elizabeth as stipulated in the will of plantation owners Robert Hugh Munro and Caleb Dickenson. It was renamed Munro College during World War I as part of the general rejection of German names at that time.

Munro took its name from one of its benefactors and was established in the fashion of the British public schools. Several of the boarding houses took the names of other benefactors or illustrious alumni. The campus features a chapel and magnificent views of the Caribbean Sea and Pedro Plains from its perch atop the Santa Cruz Mountains.

Munro has long distinguished itself as a center for excellence in secondary education in Jamaica and the Eastern Caribbean and is reputed to have produced the most Rhodes Scholars of any secondary school in the entire Caribbean. Munro is currently the only all-boys boarding school in Jamaica. It still has five houses: Pearman Calder, Coke Farquharson, Dickenson (my house), Harrison, and Sangster.

Munro presented a radical shift from the way of life I had known growing up in Burnt Savannah. The school was run in military style by senior students called prefects who ran the students' day-to-day activities from dorm life to breakfast, lunch, dinner, and study time. Prefects also ensured the rules were followed and that discipline was administered. Serious issues were handled by dorm masters (teachers) or by the principal or vice principal.

My early weeks at Munro reminded me of Hogwarts of Harry Potter fame—frightening and mysterious at the same time. As a twelve-year-old kid moving away from home for the first time, it was a tough transition, but coming from a strict family that respected rules made that transition easier.

September 1991 was my first day at Munro, a day filled with anticipation, anxiety, and fear. Watching my mother trudge down that hilly slope to find a taxi was gut-wrenching. The memory of the tears welling up in my eyes and the sinking feeling inside are still fresh. But I knew I had to be a man and make it on my own even though I was only twelve.

Once my mom left me on that bleak September day it was initiation time. Those rites of passage were carried out by the senior boys for about the first three months. Munro was about discipline. You were told when to get up, when to eat, when to study, and how to dress, and those policies were strictly enforced. Any bad behavior was quickly addressed. Classes were not for the weak-minded. You either kept up the pace, or you were left behind. The choice was yours.

Munro brought new friends and new adventures; it was a dream opportunity for me. I was introduced to a massive library and many sports. After a few weeks I started settling into my new way of life. I learned about who I was, and the doors started opening—or so I thought.

Athletics

My lanky frame at twelve was new for me and presented some challenges. In the summer of 1991 I reached new heights, and by the time I arrived at Munro on September 2, I was the tallest kid in the first form (grade seven), but my coordination was lacking. That did not prevent me from trying out for several teams. I tried out for the Under-14 cricket team but did not make it. Then I tried out for goalkeeper on the Under-14 football team, but I still had no success. I tried to make the track team but failed again, so I took up tennis, but I didn't make that team either.

My first year at Munro was an athletic disaster, but that did not deter me from continuing to try. With Munro being a boarding school, weekends provided plenty of opportunities to become a better athlete. There was no quitting. Like Rocky, I kept on fighting.

By the time Sports Day rolled around at Munro College in 1992 I was thinking that, because of my height, I could make my Dickenson House dorm team in the high jump even though I didn't know a thing about high jumping. I successfully cleared the first few heights using the scissor technique, but then I fell off the mat and badly hurt my ankle. That was the end of my Sports Day. I don't remember what position I finished.

When Sports Day 1993 arrived I was in the second form (eighth grade), and I was asked to run the 400 and 800 meters. The 400 meters was first. I was wearing cut-off jeans that were not especially suitable for running. The gun went off, and I shot forward like a bullet. At 300 meters I realized I was about 40 meters ahead of the field. I kept on running. With about 50 meters to go I looked around, and I was still way ahead. No one was challenging me. It was about to be one the biggest upsets of the day as I was running against more established and accomplished runners, but with only 5 meters to go, things went black.

When I saw the light again, I was under a tent and was being administered to. I was dehydrated and wearing improper gear, a combination that had caused me to blackout. I asked what happened and was told I had failed to make the finish line. You can only imagine how I felt when I heard that news.

I finished the day running the 800 meters and finished well. You would have thought that I would be applauded for running the 800 meters at all after passing out in the 400 only an hour earlier, but that was not the case. My 400-meter failure made me the brunt of many unkind jokes, and I was frequently reminded what a disappointment I was. Nonetheless, I did make the school track team that year in the 800 meters. But afterward, I was advised by some people to give up athletics (track). I became discouraged and stopped running, but Munro's large campus and my love for track kept me close to the sport but at a safe distance from the ridicule.

Munro's track was located at the bottom of a beautiful hill, maybe a half- mile trek from the top. There were three football fields side by side. The circle for throwing the shot was to the northwest side of the football (soccer) field, while the discus circles were at another field to the southwest of the three main football fields. Most evenings after class I would stand by the shot-put circle and watch the track team practice, and that is how a shot-putter named Nigel "Sharlo" Green started asking me to fetch the shot after he would throw it. It wasn't long before I was taking the shots to the field and waiting for him. While I waited I began experimenting with throwing the shot myself. I enjoyed it, and I was encouraged to throw the discus as well. Before I knew it, I was throwing both the shot and the discus and doing well.

My friend Prince Gareth Waite soon began accompanying me to the shot-put circle to fetch the shot after I threw it. Having someone to help and encourage me made a world of difference. I also must mention that Dickinson House had one of the most talented sprinters ever to walk the hills of Munro and Jamaica, Mr. Clive Williams, who fared well in inter-dorm sports; he was something special. I was hoping he would take his amazing athletic talents to international competition, but he chose not to. But come Sports Day, my dorm could always rely on him. He was not only a great athlete, but he was one of the kindest boys I've ever known. He also was famous as the guy who ran with a bandana in his mouth. What a talent he was.

By Sports Day 1994 my athletic abilities were developing, and I was becoming a pretty good discus thrower and shot-putter. I enjoyed practicing both events, sometimes for hours at a time on the weekends because I could be by myself. Because of my height and speed, I made the Under-16 football team as right back. I also made the Under-16 cricket team, but my focus was on conquering the shot and discuss. I competed in the shot put and finished second behind Rory Marsh, Jamaica's leading junior thrower and a year my senior. I also finished third in the discus and third in the 800 meters.

As a member of the Munro track team I then competed at the Western Champs and the Boys Championships. I had no interest in running the 800 meters other than for my dorm to gain points on Sports Day. To my surprise, I was only selected to run the 800 meters for Munro. How could that have happened? I was deeply upset. After all, I had finished in the top three of both throwing events but was not given a chance to represent my school in either one. Despite my disappointment, I ran the 800 meters.

Chapter Three

A New Journey

On Sports Day 1995 I represented my dorm again and finished second in both the shot put and discus. That also was the year I learned about the CARIFTA Games, a competition held every year throughout the Caribbean that featured the top athletes from all English-speaking countries in the region, and it included Under-17 and Under-19 divisions. I was Under-17 and Rory Marsh, Jamaica's top junior thrower, was a year older, so he competed in the Under-19 division.

Entry forms were filled out and sent to the meet organizers, and I was excited for the opportunity to represent Munro and, possibly, earn a chance to represent Jamaica. On the day we were to leave I walked up to get on the bus, but I was informed by the track coach that I would not be making the trip after all because there were other athletes with more potential. I was heartbroken. But as I turned to leave, Rory Marsh and Elston Cawley, our team captain, stepped in and convinced the track coach to let me go, and he conceded.

I believe that incident occurred because I had emerged as a strong challenger to Rory's athletic dominance. Rory and his family had always treated me with respect and dignity, which was one of the reasons for my early success in the throws. But I was treated with contempt by some students—and even a few teachers—for becoming a threat to him.

At Jamaica's National Stadium in Kingston, my first discus throw of the competition was my best of the year. I finished fourth and had to wait anxiously for two weeks to know if I would be selected to represent Jamaica at the CARIFTA Games in Georgetown, Cayman Islands.

Boys Championships
The Championships began as a sports competition between six of Jamaica's

oldest high schools: Munro College, St. George's College, Jamaica College, the Wolmer's School, New College, and Mandeville Middle-Grade School. Originally known as the Inter-Secondary School Sports Championships, rules and staging of the event were managed by an organizing committee comprising the headmasters of the six boys' schools. It was first chaired by William Cowper, headmaster of Wolmer's. The first Boys' Champs began at the famous test cricket ground of Sabina Park on June 29, 1910, in Kingston. Boys Champs was modeled after the track and field competitions at British public schools, and the event quickly gained popularity among Jamaica's sports-loving public. For the first several years fans had attended a track meet in which athletes were given handicaps according to age, reputation, and overall appearance—as in a horse race—but that format was discontinued in 1910 when new rules and a new trophy were introduced.

The Girls' Athletics Championships may have started as early as 1914 in Kingston, but that event was not continuous and only reemerged under different organizations in the 1940s. The girls' event has enjoyed an unbroken run since 1961.

Only sixteen schools have ever won a boys' or girls' championship with Kingston College (1962–1975) boasting the longest boys' winning streak and Vere Technical holding the longest girls' winning streak (1979–1993). In a hundred years, only Excelsior High School and St. Jago High have ever won both boys' and girls' divisions at Champs. The feat has never been accomplished in the same year. Munro has won the Boys' Championships eight times, but none since 1948.

The week before the Boys Championships it was announced that I would be representing Jamaica in the CARIFTA Games, and only two of us from Munro had been selected. Elston Cawley would join me. What some at Munro had said was impossible had become a reality: I had made my first Jamaican national team.

Boys Champs 1995 was filled with anticipation. I was at the stadium's dusty grass track warming up with my teammate Rory while my other teammate, Sheldon Lewis, looked on. I was one of the favorites to win the shot put event and challenge Rory for dominance. I also was predicted to finish in a top spot for the discus. Things were looking great. I had been selected to Jamaica's CARIFTA team and was ready to compete for a medal at Boys Champs. That was every Jamaican track and field athlete's dream—to win a medal at Boys Championships, but I was in for a surprise.

When the events were called and the athletes presented themselves to the event marshal, before moving onto the field of competition I presented myself only to be told I was not entered in the event.

"That cannot be true; it must be a mistake," I said. "How is this possible?" I cried my heart out. Somehow, I had not been entered into the discus event—only the 800 meters—an event in which I had not even the slightest chance of advancing beyond the first round. I had not even been training for it. I had proven myself one of the best throwers in my age category in all of Jamaica and was good enough to make Jamaica's national team, but I was not good enough to make my high school team, which needed all the points it could get. I was gutted.

Most people were mystified by the situation, but I felt the reason I was left off was that I was not highly regarded as an athlete at Munro. I did not have the traditional pedigree. The talent I possessed needed to be molded patiently, and I did not have the right look or fit the script of the ideal athlete. And beyond all that, I was not from an affluent family. To his shock, my teammate Sheldon Lewis was entered to compete alongside Rory Marsh. But Lewis withdrew from the event because he believed what had been done to me was unfair. I was allowed to compete at the last minute, but by then the damage had been done. I failed to make the final, and that was the end of Boys Champs for me.

* * *

"Keep your head tucked behind your helmet!" my dad shouted as the motorcycle hit 80 mph as it zoomed through the traffic along Mandela Highway in St. Catherine. We were headed to the passport office on Spanish Town Road because I needed a passport to travel to the Cayman Islands for the CARIFTA Games. The office closed at five, and it was already 4:30 on Friday evening. My documents needed to be in before the close of the day. Knowing my dad, he would do everything possible to make sure I was on that plane to the Cayman Islands the upcoming week. We made it to the passport office with minutes to spare. I was issued a temporary passport good enough to travel and would receive a permanent one later, so I was all set.

"Welcome to Air Jamaica!" the pilot announced as we took off from the Norman Manley International Airport in Kingston. I looked across at my teammates dressed in Jamaica's national colors of black, gold, and green as the plane climbed to cruising altitude. I could feel bubbles in my belly as the plane cleared the clouds and gave way to beautiful sunshine.

I did not have much of a conversation with my teammates on our short flight as most of my focus was on the beauty of the ocean below. Childhood memories came rushing back of the many times I had seen planes flying high above my home and had wondered where they were going. Now I was on one of those planes myself and headed to a whole new world. My daydreaming was cut short as the pilot announced our descent into Georgetown, capital of the Caymans.

The Cayman Islands is a beautiful country with friendly people. The atmosphere at the hotel was great, and I enjoyed the food.

I also enjoyed meeting athletes from different countries and learning about their cultures firsthand rather than from a book.

The Games themselves began on April 15, 1995, and I was wearing Jamaica's national colors at Truman Bodden Stadium in Georgetown, a far cry from the playground in Burnt Savannah or the hills of Munro. The first final was the boys' Under-17 shot put, and the first thrower was none other than me, Claston Anthony Bernard. On my first throw I set a stadium record and became the first gold medalist in the brand-new stadium. The world to new possibilities had been opened; I was a Jamaican gold medalist.

When our Jamaican team returned home, we were welcomed as heroes. I could not wait to show my family my gold medal, and they were proud.

* * *

It was Sports Day 1996 at Munro, and my dorm had become dominant in track and football. I decided to take on more events to earn more points for my dorm, so I entered the 100, 200, and 400 meters as well as the shot and discus. I was with the big boys. I was no longer an Under-17 athlete and would have to prove myself at the new level. I did better than was expected, finishing second behind new star athlete Dwhyte Barrett in both the 100 and 200 meters. That surprised many people, although it shouldn't have as I had proven to be one of the fastest football players at Munro.

Due to my commitment to the throws, I was unable to compete in the 400 meters, so I ran on the 4x100 relay team instead. At the Western Champs that year I was second in both throwing events. At the 1996 CARIFTA Games trials I finished third in both the shot put and the discus. My selection to represent Jamaica at the twenty-sixth staging of the games rested on the selection committee. As it turned out, they opted for more experienced and senior athletes. Though I was disappointed,

I realized the committee's decision was fair, so I could live with it. At the Boys' Championships I was second in the shot put and fifth in the discus. That wrapped up my track season for 1996.

* * *

"Stay back in the center of the circle, Longas." That's what Dr. Kevin Gwyn Jones called me. "Stay focused and slow things down."

My journey to throwing success did not happen all by myself. I was guided under the watchful eyes of Dr. Jones, a man who dedicated his life to success and helping Munro throwers and jumpers improve. Gwyn, as we affectionately called him, would volunteer to help develop our throwing abilities on weekends. With him believing in me and guiding me along the way, I gained the added confidence I needed to succeed. He saw my raw talent and took on the challenge of molding me into one of the Caribbean's top throwers.

Then there was Mr. Marsh, Rory's dad, who not only focused on his son's development but was an encouraging factor in my early success in the throwing events as well. There are not enough pages to say thank you to those two men, both of whom invested their time, their money, and their faith in me when others told me to quit.

* * *

I was in the third form (ninth grade) when I heard a voice call out, "Hey, young man!" as I walked under the arches at Munro below Coke Farquharson's dorm on the way back from one of my favorite places, the dining room. I turned to see who was calling me, but it was not someone I was familiar with. I strolled over to two gentlemen with my lanky 6' 4", 175-pound frame, and they introduced themselves as Mr. Laurie Sharp (LW) and Trevor Armstrong. Mr. Sharp was the chairman of the Munro College Old Boys Association while Mr. Armstrong was a board member.

Mr. Sharp wanted to know what I was doing with that lanky frame of mine. LW had a great passion for the game of cricket, and he wanted to know if I was still playing. I told him I was but that my interests included running track and playing football. He was direct with his questions and wanted to know what plans I had to make my goals a reality. I told him what I would like to accomplish as an athlete, and I must have left an impression on both men because they have been two of my biggest supporters ever since.

Mr. Sharp gave me direction that I would not have received from many people. My parents had dreams for all their children to escape poverty, and they knew that education was the vehicle, so they gave us all they could and more, but they did not know what to do once we had acquired our basic education. But Mr. Sharp was there to sow the seeds that would grow into a launching pad for my future.

Chapter Four

A New Purpose

I used to stand in our school's dining room and study all the names of Munro's most decorated students on the scholarship boards and wonder how I could have my name up there.

Elston Cawley, Munro's head prefect, was in Dickenson House, and he was a phenomenal athlete who competed for Jamaica in the 1996 Atlanta Olympic Games, making it to the quarterfinals of the 200 meters. He also attended the University of Texas-Arlington on a track scholarship.

"A track scholarship?" I wondered to myself. I had no idea such a thing was possible. You mean I could get a scholarship for track and earn a university education? Until then I thought only the brightest students could earn scholarships and attend universities. I did not realize that some of the guys on the boards were able to use their athletic skills to get them into some of the best foreign universities to further their academic studies as well as to pursue their athletic dreams.

To add intrigue to my new-found revelation I was given a book by a friend whose dad, Kurt Betton Jr., was a doctor. The book was titled *Gifted Hands* and told the story of a boy named Ben Carson who rose from destitute poverty in America to become one of the best neurosurgeons the world has ever seen. The lights started coming on. Even though we were so many miles apart, Carson's story was similar to mine. That's when I started plotting my next move. Often we go about things because we are told they will make our lives better, but there are no guide books. How do you move from A to B? How do you change B into reality, and how do you silence the voices of negativity?

The summer of 1996 brought the Olympic Games to Atlanta, Georgia. I was newly inspired with the dream of one day competing in that greatest of all global sporting events. My focus was on how to go about attracting an athletic scholarship that would help me compete in the Olympics.

* * *

It was about five in the morning one day in the fall of 1996. It was dark and misty on the Munro campus as the eerie shrieks of the wind and the wailing of the willow trees echoed through the three stories of Dickenson House. I slipped out of my pajamas and into my track suit as my dormmates slept. I grabbed my sneakers, covered in red dirt, and darted down the stairs into the crisp, chilly morning air as my body shivered in the cold.

You might be surprised to learn that it gets cold in tropical Jamaica, but with Munro College sitting high in the Santa Cruz Mountains, the temperature can easily drop into the 50s, especially when it's windy. My run would be the three-mile trek through Mother Blair's Hill. Those were special moments for me because I could think and reflect on life in general. Yes, those runs taught me much about life. They became a ritual, and as my drive to succeed became clearer, my hunger for those runs became even deeper. I wanted to go where no one believed I could go, and I had a burning drive and a new purpose in getting there.

The fall of 1996 also saw a much-needed boost to Munro's track and field program with the addition of Leroy Allison as head coach. Mr. Allison breathed new life into Munro's track program and gave it a new vision. It was as if the invisible hand was putting all the pieces of my life's puzzle together.

When I met Coach Allison I told him what my plans were and what I would like to accomplish in track. I don't know if he would remember, but I also told him I wanted to be on the scholarship board in Munro's dining hall. His first conversation with me focused on my academic performance. He then laid out what was needed to help me accomplish my goals.

By 1998 I had earned all the necessary academic qualifications except for a science credit. But without science, I would have to go to a Division II school in the United States, a second-tier athletic program, and then transfer to a major university with a top athletic program. Munro had a tradition of excellence, and I wanted to continue that tradition by going to a major college program from the start.

I set my sights on going to a top-tier university in Division-1A, but to accomplish that I had to take three years of Human and Social Biology in about three months. I hadn't taken any biology in four years, but Coach Allison was also Munro's A-Level (advanced) biology teacher, and he committed himself to teaching me and another athlete, Sean Parris, who would go on to Tulane University in Louisiana on a track scholarship.

Coach Allison taught us for about three hours a night after we finished our mandatory study sessions. Munro required all students to spend an hour- and-a-half to two hours a night studying and doing homework. Because I had met all other requirements, all I needed was a C in the biology course to qualify for a scholarship to an American Division 1A university. But being able to meet those requirements did not happen by accident. It could be considered a miracle that my new track coach was an expert teacher in the exact subject I needed. How could that have happened? It may have been impossible anywhere else. An invisible hand once again seemed to have intervened on my behalf.

* * *

The Munro College grounds overlook the beautiful Pedro Plains, the site of Sports Day 1997. I was set to compete in about seven events as captain of my dorm team. We needed all the points we could get to defend our title. One of our best middle- and long-distance runners—one of the best Munro has ever produced—also was one of my best friends. We were so close he was almost a member of the family. Gareth Prince Waite went on to study at the University of Mona Campus in Jamaica. His only interest in track was at the recreational level. He didn't see much of a future in it beyond high school.

Another dormmate and friend, Noel Comrie, was one of the best triple jumpers to attend Munro. He also was a good all-around athlete who helped spur Dickenson to another inter-dorm championship. I was named the meet's most outstanding athlete, which I considered recognition of my hard work and dedication.

Following Sports Day, Coach Allison called me to his office and asked if I had ever considered participating in the heptathlon, a seven-event competition contested at the Boys Championships until the decathlon was introduced several years after my graduation. I had no idea what the heptathlon was or what events it included. Coach Allison explained that it consisted of the (1) 110 meter hurdles, (2) high jump, (3) shot put, (4) 200 meters, (5) long jump, (6) discus, and (7) 1500 meters.

My first response was, "No way! That is crazy!" I didn't know how to high jump or long jump, let alone hurdle. Munro did not even have hurdles, and worst of all, the 1500 meters was too painful of an event. But Coach Allison then calmly pointed out that the heptathlon was contested over two days, and I had just competed in seven events in only one day at Sports Day, winning most of them. He had a point. But could I do it at the Boys Championships less than two months away?

I had the Western Champs and the National Field Events Champs coming up soon. I was the top thrower in the country and would be running the 100 meters and 200 meters along with the 4x100 meter relay at the Western Champs. I would go on to win both throws with a record in the shot put and finished second in the 100 meters and third in the 200 meters.

Finally, I decided to take my head coach's offer and started preparing to compete in the heptathlon at the Boys Championships. My first task was to learn the high and long jumps. Munro was blessed to have in its services one of the most talented all-round athletes Jamaica has ever produced, Paul "Pablo T" Thompson. He was long jumping over 25 feet by the time he was fifteen and was jumping over 6 feet in the high jump while also being a sprinting phenom. I was to partner with him to learn the jumps.

In our first session together I jumped 6' 4", which was the challenge Pablo T had issued. At that time I was 6' 4" and about 190 pounds. As you can tell, I caught onto the high jump and long jump quickly, my speed and power serving as great assets in both events. But the hurdles were a different story.

The National Field Events and Hurdles Champs was held at National Stadium in Kingston in front of a packed grandstand. Before the event I had built one hurdle in Munro's woodwork shop so I could practice. I was in a heat with accomplished hurdlers who also would be doing the heptathlon at the Boys Championships about two weeks later. But this was the first test Mr. Allison believed I had to overcome to challenge for supremacy in the heptathlon, an event dominated by Kingston's urban schools.

Standing behind my blocks I was nervous with anticipation as we were called to the starting line. The stadium fell silent. The starter raised his gun and, as he fired, we were off. I was the first out and led at the first hurdle, but that was when things changed. I had no idea how to measure my steps after that first hurdle so, upon reaching the second one, I backed up and did a high jump scissor move, and I repeated that for every remaining hurdle. Halfway through the race I could hear pandemonium in the stadium. At least half the people were laughing hysterically. I tried my best to shut out the crowd and complete the task I had started. As I crossed the finish line I saw some of my teammates, and they were laughing too.

For some in the stadium my first attempt at the hurdles had been entertaining, but for others it had been ridiculous. I could hear their negative comments. Many said I had been a major embarrassment, but I considered it a major victory. I had done what my coach had asked of me. Mr. Allison later told me he never thought I would attempt the race given that I had only practiced going over one hurdle.

I think a video of the race was available at one time, but I was not the least embarrassed by it and was not ashamed for trying. I had learned to overcome embarrassments a long time before. What I did not know was that Coach Allison was preparing me for the ten events of the decathlon.

* * *

It was March 1997, time for the Boys Championships at the Kingston National Stadium. The events I entered were the shot put, discus, 4x100 meter relay, and the heptathlon. Once again I found myself at the starting line for the heptathlon's 110-meter hurdles. Two weeks before, you will recall, I had made my first attempt at hurdling and had become the talk of the town—and some rural areas as well.

Leading up to the championships I was still one of the favorites to win the heptathlon if I could finish the hurdles with a decent time because I was strong in all the other events. For the two weeks after that first hurdle race I had spent every second I could going over the hurdles and learning as much as I could about the event.

The starter called us to our marks and raised his gun. While poised on my mark I remember looking all the way through the hurdles to the finish line and remembering the words of the poet Henry Wadsworth

Longfellow: "The heights by great men reached and kept / Were not attained by sudden flight, but they, while their companions slept, were toiling upward in the night." My goal was to reach that finish line. The field of hurdlers included most of the guys I had competed against two weeks earlier.

The gun went off, and again I was first out of the blocks like a flash and found myself alone at the first hurdle and then the second, expecting a surge from the rest of the field, but none ever came. Before I knew it, I was first to the finish line to the amazement and shock of all who were present. "How could that have happened?" someone marveled aloud.

I had accomplished the impossible, and the laughter of two weeks earlier had been replaced by stunned disbelief. By the time all the events were finished I had broken the heptathlon meet record, won the discus, finished second in the shot put, and anchored Munro to sixth place in the

4x100 meter finals. To top it off, I was voted the most outstanding athlete of the championships. In addition, Munro College finished in the top five for the first time in many years. Munro track and field had been reborn.

I can also say that I had come to appreciate running the 800 meters all those years, even if I had started as the result of bad judgment by my coach, because it had kept me active in my throwing years and helped the transition to the 1500 meters that I would run later in the decathlon. Running the 800 meters, even though disappointing at the time, paid off in the end.

My 1997 season ended as I represented Jamaica in Bridgetown, Barbados, at the CARIFTA Games in the shot put (third) and discus (fourth). And was wrapped up in Havana, Cuba, for the Panam-Games.

Chapter Five

The Decathlon

The word "decathlon" is of Greek origin. In track and field, the decathlon is a series of ten events held over two consecutive days. The winner is determined by a points system based on performance in each of the ten events.

The unofficial title of "World's Greatest Athlete" traditionally has been given to the person who wins the Olympic decathlon. That tradition began when King Gustav V of Sweden told Jim Thorpe, "You, sir, are the world's greatest athlete" after Thorpe, a native American of the Sac and Fox Nation, won the decathlon at the Stockholm Olympics in 1912.

The vast majority of international and top-level men's decathlon events are organized in the order below:

Day 1 – 100 meters, long jump, shot put, high jump, and 400 meters

Day 2 – 110-meter hurdles, discus, pole vault, javelin, and 1500 meters

Jamaica gave me the opportunity to compete in the decathlon in the summer of 1997 at the Pan American Games in Havana, Cuba, because I had already qualified in the shot put. But I had no idea of how to pole vault or throw the javelin and, to make matters worse, Munro had no such equipment.

I was determined to learn the pole vault and javelin anyway. Traveling to Kingston so I could use proper equipment was out of the question; it was too far, so I started using the high jump mats at the end of our long jump pit as a makeshift pole vault pit. The sand would soften the falls each time I would miss the mats. For the javelin, I started using a stick to practice my basic throwing technique.

The decathlon was not only a new event for me but for Jamaica. I had never heard of anyone who had seriously attempted to train for the decathlon at the highest levels. This was the dream of a lifetime. I finished seventh in my first attempt at the decathlon without clearing a single height in the pole vault. Using the proper poles was too difficult, and I barely threw over twenty meters in the javelin. Even though weak in those two events, I was still able to score 5,998 points at the Pan-Am Games on my first try, and that wrapped up my 1997 track and field season.

The 1998 season began with me dominating the throws and the high jump. I had become a household name in Jamaica track and field, and foreign universities had begun taking notice. I was overwhelmed with the number of scholarship offers I was receiving. I addition to throwing, I became one of Munro's main sprinters in the 4x100 meter relay and the 4x400 meter relay as well. Munro had produced one of the fastest times that year in the 4x400—4 minutes and 13 seconds—with me running the leadoff leg.

The pressure was mounting on me to stay focused on the decathlon because 1998 was also the year of the World Junior Championships to be held in Annecy, France. I dominated the throws that year and had become one of the top high jumpers in high school, but I only focused on the throws, the relays, and the heptathlon at the Boys Championships because I had a full plate.

By the end of the Boys Championships I had set another heptathlon record and was again named most outstanding athlete. Not bad for a kid who had been told he had no chance to be successful competing against the boys from Kingston. Also, I later learned that I was featured on the cover of the 1999 edition of the newly combined Boys and Girls Championships publication.

Munro finished in the top five again, a big deal for a school without the size advantages of the urban schools and even many rural ones. Munro's high academic standards and the costs of competition would not allow its teams to compete against the larger schools for Champs supremacy.

After Boys Champs 1998 I had two primary tasks to complete. First was to pass biology and second was to qualify for the World Junior Championships. The route to the World Juniors would go through the Central American Champs (CAC) held in July in the Cayman Islands. The pinnacle for any junior athlete—besides the Olympic Games—is to compete at the World Junior Championships where most future Olympians are born. I only had one shot at qualifying, and I not only needed to win, I needed to score above 6,600 points. I was still weak in the pole vault and javelin, which made the task that much more difficult. I remember writing these words in my track diary in 1998: "I will always aim high to reach the top. It's a long way, but I can reach it."

At Munro my focus was on tying up the loose ends. I wanted to attend a top American university and had narrowed my sights to Louisiana State University (LSU). Mr. Allison had prepared me well for the biology exam, but I would have to wait until the end of the summer to know if I passed and could qualify for a major college scholarship. I said my goodbyes to Munro College and the city on a hill that is forever etched in my heart; it was time to move on. I had to focus on the upcoming CAC Games and qualifying for the World Junior Champs.

* * *

At about 30,000 feet I took the headphones out of the packet and plugged them into the armrest as I headed for Annecy, France. When I slipped the headphones over my ears I heard the voice of Bill Medley singing, "I've had the time of my life. No, I never felt this way before. Yes, I swear it's the truth." He was singing a 1987 song composed by Franke Previte,

John DeNicola, and Donald Markowitz that had been used as the theme for the 1987 film *Dirty Dancing*. And I was having the time of my life too.

At the World Junior Championships in France I was in fourth place until the javelin and pole vault. Those events sent me to a thirteenth-place finish despite setting a Jamaica national decathlon record of 6,769 points. That was a new frontier for me and Jamaica, and a dream well realized.

The results of my test in Human and Social Biology were supposed to have arrived before I left for the World Junior Championships, but they did not, and I could not start college without that science credit. At the conclusion of the games, my Munro teammate Lueroy Colquhoun moved to LSU as both of us had been offered full scholarships there. The semester was about to start, and my anxiety increased.

Summer ended and school had already started when I finally received a call from LSU Coach Mark Elliot. He said I had been given the OK by the NCAA Clearinghouse to attend LSU. "You passed Human and Social Biology with a grade of B," the coach said. "Gather your things and come on up."

Chapter Six

Louisiana State University

"You will never make it at LSU. They do not take good care of their athletes." That was only one of the many voices dissuading me from heading north on a track scholarship. In the spring of 1997 I had taken my visit to LSU and had been highly impressed with its program. Led by the Legendary Pat Henry, LSU had talent in all areas I was interested in. In addition, Coach Irving "Boo" Schexnayder was armed with an arsenal of information to help his athletes improve. All of that drew me to LSU where I would be allowed to develop and not be expected to take on the responsibilities of the star athlete right away.

I turned to Mr. Larry (LW) Sharp, whose advice I valued highly. He assured me I should follow my dreams, but I should make sure I knew what I wanted to study and stick with it. That was all I needed to hear. I had the full support of my parents who wanted the best for me, and they also had come to trust Mr. Sharp's advice.

My oldest sister Andrea purchased my plane ticket, and my family gave me all the money they could spare. I said my goodbyes and set off with my bags like Dick Whittington and his cat, only this time, to the chime of LSU's clock.

It was already two weeks into the 1998 fall semester at LSU when I finally left Kingston, Jamaica, early in the morning and arrived at the Baton Rouge airport around 5 p.m. I was picked up by my friend and old schoolmate Dwhyte Barrett who was studying engineering and, like me, running track at LSU on a full scholarship. He took me straight to my Music Appreciation class that met at 6 p.m. that same evening. It was a three-hour class, an elective for my degree in Human Resource Management. Because I knew what I wanted to study, I had been able to select my classes before I arrived on the LSU campus. Coming from a school like Munro College with its rigorous academic program made the transition to university life easy. It was time for a new chapter, and I was ready.

Freshman Season at LSU

My fall training was one of adjustments as Coach Boo Schexnayder's focus was to get me technically sound and coordinated. Coach Boo, as we called him, was especially adept at track and field's multiple events. A product of Louisiana himself, he guided many of LSU's jumpers to stellar careers. Some of his top athletes included Olympians Jamaica's Suzette Lee and Kiesha Spencer, both NCAA triple jump champs and record holders. He helped Russ Buller clear over 19 feet in the pole vault and win NCAA and South Eastern Conference (SEC) titles.

He also guided Levar Anderson to NCAA titles and, later, my teammate at LSU, Walter Davis, became world triple jump champion and one of the greatest athletes

Louisiana has ever produced in the jumps and sprints. Coach Boo also helped stellar long and triple jumper Marcus Thomas and Olympic silver medalist John Moffitt as well LSU standout Lejuan Simon. Coach Boo was Level 1 and II certified by USA Track and Field and also was a biomechanics instructor for USA Track and Field. He knew what he was doing, and his new task was to develop me into a top decathlete.

My freshman bio at LSU read like this: Prep Career: A tremendous raw talent who may blossom into a fantastic athlete. . . Qualified for the World Junior Championships in Annecy, France, this past summer. . . His versatility is witnessed through two events he won at the World Juniors—the high jump and the discuss. . . finished 13th at World Juniors, won the CAC gold medal in the decathlon and was gold, silver, and bronze medalist at the CARIFTA Games between 1995-98. . . also an accomplished soccer and cricket player.

That was what I had to live up to at LSU.

I entered the 1999 indoor season after a good fall training, and I had to get up to speed with indoor competition, something new to me. The NCAA did not schedule the multi-events indoors, so I competed mainly in the high jump, long jump, 60-meter hurdles, and running the 400-meter leg of LSU's distance medley relay (DMR) team, which finished fourth at the SEC with a season-best time.

Outdoor season 1999
Two weeks into the outdoor season I injured my ankle so badly that surgery was recommended, but I refused. Instead, I decided to go through the difficult rehab process. I did not want to be out for the rest of my freshman year and was looking forward to competing in the decathlon.

My first event back from injury was the decathlon at the Texas Relays in Austin. The conditions were pretty bad—rain, cold, and high winds—and to make matters worse, I was still nursing my ankle. Even so, I finished second in the open decathlon, my first as a collegian, with a personal best of 6,840 points. I was able to save my outdoor season and moved my focus to the SEC Championships scheduled for Athens, Georgia. At the SEC event I became only the second freshman to win the decathlon with a then personal best of 7,444 points, a Jamaican national record, and a 604-point improvement from two weeks earlier while still nursing my ankle.

I had set personal bests in nine events: the 100 meters, long jump, shot put, high jump, 400 meters, hurdles, pole vault, and javelin and, in the process, had moved to number seven on LSU's all-time decathlon list. I followed that performance with a fifth-place finish at the NCAA event two weeks later in the cold and rain of Boise, Idaho, with 7,395 points. I earned freshman All-American honors after going into the meet ranked eleventh, and I was the only freshman to qualify in the decathlon that year. LSU labeled it one of the greatest accomplishments in LSU and SEC track and field history.

Sophomore Season

The year 2000 was an Olympic year with the games set for Sydney, Australia, that fall, and I was dreaming of becoming an Olympian for Jamaica. Never before had anyone represented Jamaica at the Olympic level, and my dream was to change history. The target was 7,706 points to qualify, but my personal best was only 7,444.

I opened the indoor season with a third-place finish in the SEC high jump. My first decathlon for the season would be at Texas A&M University in College Station where I set a personal best of 7,536 points. I followed that with my second SEC title with a score over 7,600 points that was agonizingly close to but still short of the Olympic requirement, but I had one more shot.

That shot came at Duke University in Durham, North Carolina. With temperatures soaring, you could feel the steam coming off the track; it was sizzling. I came into that meet with high expectations of qualifying for the Sydney Olympic Games, but things were not looking good in that scorching heat. My first two events didn't go well and, with an ice pack on the back of my neck, I remember Coach Boo pulling me aside and telling me to get it together. "You have a dream," he said, "one that can still be realized."

I was down, but that talk inspired me, and I came up with a strong performance in the shot put, high jumped a personal best of 6' 11" and ran a decathlon 400 meters best of 48.22 seconds.

The second day started well with me in the lead and the gap widening—
until the pole vault. I missed my first two attempts at 12' 6" and was in danger of no height, which would have been the end of

both my shot at the NCAA title and my Olympic dream. With my nerves frayed, I decided to pass on my last attempt at the opening height and take my final effort at the next height so I would have more time to gather myself.

With the bar set at 13' 2", my heart was pounding as the announcer called "Bernard up!" I walked slowly to my run marker, picked up my pole, took a deep breath, and set off down the runway. "Plant high" I remember telling myself. "Plant high!" And I remember my teammate and training partner Russ Buller, one of LSU's and America's most decorated pole vaulters, yelling as he cheered me on while I sprinted down the runway. I hit the mat and heard the roar of the crowd. I had done it. I had flown over the bar! My NCAA title hopes and Olympic dream were still alive.

Plenty of work remained. I was passed by Bevan Heart of the University of California after his brilliant pole vault, so I had to work hard in the javelin to stay on course to qualify for the Olympics. I was in second place going into the decathlon's final event, the 1500 meters. I had to run it in under 4 minutes and 50 seconds, which was easy under normal circumstances. After all, as my personal best was 4:36, but the situation at Duke was anything but ordinary with the heat making the 1500 meters a blistering challenge.

* * *

The plane took off from Baton Rouge that early August morning: destination, Brisbane, Australia, to join Jamaica's Olympic camp. That was an exciting time for me. As you can guess, I had made the score necessary to qualify for the Olympics. In the final event of that NCAA decathlon in June I had run the 1500 meters in 4:44 to finish second overall with 7,806 points, a full 100 points over the Olympic qualifying mark. I became the second athlete from Burnt Savannah to make it to the Olympic Games, and the first for Jamaica. The other Olympian from

Burnt Savannah was British Javelin gold medalist Tessa Sanderson who had left Burnt Savannah at an early age and competed for Great Britain from 1976 to 1996. She, too, had been a heptathlete.

On Wednesday, September 27, 2000, I marched into the Olympic Stadium in Sydney to the applause of over 70,000. It was a dream come true. I was on the largest stage, the Olympic Games, a reality that had seemed impossible only four years earlier. I had done it. I had arrived. How did a guy who had not been given a chance to succeed or to even leave his home make it to the greatest athletic competition in the world? I was only twenty-one years old.

The first event was the 100 meters. I was hungry and wanted more. The sprinters were called to our marks, the starter raised his gun, and we were off. I managed a personal best of 10.79. That was a dream start and the highlight of my career to that point. I was told the crowd had gone wild back in Jamaica.

The long jump was next, and the excitement from the 100 meters carried over, but then disaster struck. I fouled all three jumps due to inexperience and not having Coach Boo at my side. He couldn't make it to Sydney as he had to prepare LSU's other athletes for the upcoming NCAA season. I continued the competition until I fouled out in the pole vault. Even so, I was encouraged by my performances in the sprinting events, the high jump, and discus.

Junior Season 2001

To be considered a top decathlete, a score of over 8,000 points is needed, and that was my new aim. Returning from the Sydney Olympics with newly acquired experience, I started my junior season on a blaze, hungry to win my first NCAA title. I opened my first decathlon with a score of over 7,800 points at Texas A&M and was focused on winning my third SEC title in as many years.

SEC Championships – Columbia, South Carolina

I had a slow start in the 100 meters, but I had improved my long jump, high jump, and hurdles performances tremendously and did not have to rely too heavily on the sprints to make up for points I used to lose in those other three events. I was not one of the better high jumpers, although I consistently jumped over 7 feet. I enjoyed a strong first day, but it was not without drama. I stepped off the narrow high jump platform and tweaked my ankle. Fortunately, I had great trainers who helped me continue the event.

The goal was to focus on hitting the marks in each event on the second day of competition. I did, but I needed to run under 4 minutes and 38 seconds to break the 8,000-point barrier for the first time. I managed to run the 1500 meters in 4:36.84 to reach 8,024 points. I had achieved the ultimate; I had broken the 8000-point barrier and was the overwhelming favorite to win the 2001 NCAA decathlon title.

NCAA Championships in Oregon

LSU went into the meet as the favorite to win the men's title, and the first event final would be the decathlon. I was in the best shape of my collegiate career, and I had recorded one of the best scores in the world heading into the meet. I was ready to take my first NCAA title.

The weather was amazing as the athletes were called up for the first heat of the 100 meters. The gun sounded, and I was quickly in the lead. I had run a decathlon personal best of 10.61 a few weeks prior and was in great sprinting shape, but halfway through I pulled my hamstring. I made it to the finish line, but then I fell to the ground in great agony. My trainers rushed to me and did all they could to help me continue, but it was to no avail. My promising season, my hopes for my first NCAA title, and a chance to compete in my first World Championships were over. My injury also affected my team's performance as we were depending on my points to set the pace for a men's outdoor title, something LSU had not accomplished since 1990.

Senior Season 2002
There was much to look forward to in my senior year. I was on schedule to graduate in the spring with my degree in Human Resource Management, and LSU was hosting the NCAA Championships in June. How would I handle the disappointment from the injury suffered at the 2001 NCAA Championships? Was I fully recovered? Those were some of the burning questions on my mind. I wanted an individual and team NCAA title badly as the crowning moments of my collegiate career.

In 2002 officials had introduced the pentathlon—five events in one day—for the SEC indoor season after a long hiatus. At the SEC Indoor Championships in Fayetteville, Arkansas, I scored 4,350 points to win and was only 106 points shy of the pentathlon world record held by former LSU Tiger Sheldon Blockburger.

That gave me a fourth SEC title. I also finished second in the high jump and qualified for the National Indoor Championships for the first time in my collegiate career with a jump of 2.17 meters (7' 1¾"). I also recorded a personal best with a long jump of 24' 5½". I finished twelfth at those NCAA Championships in Fayetteville.

The outdoor season started on March 20 in College Station, Texas, a week after the National Indoor Championships. I opened my season with a decathlon win and a new personal best of 8,050 points. I also scored a personal best in the high jump at 7' 2", which put me in the top ten high jumpers in the country.

My focus after that season opener quickly turned to winning the elusive NCAA title at the National Championships at our own Bernie Moore Stadium in Baton Rouge. My coach and I decided it would be best not to defend my SEC outdoor title because the SEC event was too close to the NCAA

Championships, and he did not want to have a repeat of what had happened the year before with my injury. We thought that for the SECs I should focus on my four strongest events to score points for the LSU Tigers.

It was May 2002, and the SEC Outdoor Championships were underway in Starkville on the Mississippi State University campus. I had a high jump personal best of 2.19 meters, (7' 2¾") to finish second and also recorded another personal best in the 110-meter hurdles with a time of 14.13, just missing the finals. That was a great meet for me, including throwing 15.10 meters in the shot put for ninth place and scoring a modest long jump of 22' 10", but it was a good performance to prepare for the NCAAs.

Late on the evening of June 1, 2002, Bernie Moore Stadium was filled to capacity, and the crowd was bustling with excitement. The home-standing LSU Tigers were in position to claim both the men's and women's NCAA track and field titles. But the men's team title would need a win in the decathlon.

A year earlier, at the National Championships in Eugene, Oregon, I had pulled my hamstring in the first event of the decathlon and, within eleven seconds, all hopes of an NCAA team title had been dashed. Now we were lined up for the 1500 meters, and I was 43 points behind the decathlon leader, Ryan Harlan of Rice, who was turning in an excellent NCAA performance. It had been a tough second day for me after a strong first day. I was battling injuries and had suffered some bad performances, but somehow I still had a chance for the title going into the last event, but I needed to beat Harlan by at least six seconds.

We were lined up on the eastern side of the track where temporary bleachers had been erected next to the Pete Maravich Center, and those bleachers were jammed full. I remember looking into the stands for my older sister Andrea. She had come to watch me graduate with my degree in business (Human Resource Management) and to see me compete in my last collegiate meet. I remember wishing my other siblings and my parents could have been there to witness those moments too, moments four years in the making.

I had finished fifth my freshman year, second my sophomore year, and was hurt my junior year. How would my senior year end?

I could feel a slight, cool breeze mix with the warm Baton Rouge atmosphere as we were called to our marks. With my 6' 4" frame and 218 pounds, I was a far cry from my 193-pound freshman self. "This is the moment you have dreamed of," I thought. "Trust your training."

The gun went off, and so did the decathlon leader, Ryan Harlan. At 400 meters I kept pushing the pace into the second lap heading toward the main stands on the west side of the track. I heard the crowd cheering wildly. I felt them willing me to victory.

As we neared the 800-meter mark Ryan was still at my heels, and I knew it was time to separate myself from him if I wanted to win that race. The crowd roared louder and louder as we darted down the east side of the track and headed for the 1000-meter mark.

At the bell lap the crowd was going crazy. I kept pushing harder. My body ached, but I had a race to win. I remember glancing across the track and seeing Ryan on the other side and, as I entered the final turn toward the finish line, I saw the crowd was in a frenzy. My legs were heavy from the two days of competition, but that crowd and my heart willed me on. I knew the race was over.

As I crossed the finish line I raised my hands in victory and collapsed to the ground. I had beaten Ryan by more than 30 seconds and had finished the competition with a personal best of 8,094 points, a Jamaican national record, and I had put the Tigers in position to win our first outdoor title in twelve years.

That long-awaited dream had become reality, and as I climbed the podium to collect my trophy there was silence within me, a silence I could not understand. After all, I should be happy. I had just won my first NCAA title. But that night on the podium I realized that something was missing. You know that feeling you get after listening to your favorite love song, the one that will have your toes curling? There is a deep longing that wants the song to keep playing, but you know it will end. Yes, that was it. I kept thinking, "Is that all? After all the hard work, pain, sweat, and tears, there must be something else."

What was I was longing for? Whatever it was, one of my greatest wins did not provide the satisfaction I had thought it would.

Chapter Seven

Life as a Pro

The Commonwealth Games

The Commonwealth Games (known as the British Empire Games from 1930–1950, the British Empire and Commonwealth Games from 1954–1966, and the British Commonwealth Games from 1970–1974) is an international multisport event involving athletes from the Commonwealth of Nations. It has taken place every four years since its inception, except in 1942 and 1946 when the event was canceled due to World War II. It is one of the largest international sporting events outside of the Olympic Games.

Pete Coley and I sat side by side on our flight to Manchester, England; we chatted until we fell asleep on our way to the 2002 Commonwealth Games. Coley, also a product of Munro College, was two years my junior. He was an amazing sprinter and, as a nineteen-year-old, he had run the second fastest time in LSU history in the indoor 400 meters at 45.37 seconds. He followed that with a 44.62 outdoors. He was also a major player in the LSU Tigers' top-rated relay teams. Moreover, he was a friend I could always count on no matter the circumstances. We did not know what to expect at the Games, but we were excited to be members of Jamaica's team.

The games in Manchester had a similar air to that of the Olympics. There were more than 5,000 athletes competing in about 250 events. My focus was to continue my winning season and secure a long-term professional contract. I had completed a long season and simply wanted to compete with myself and not become too distracted.

The atmosphere was electrifying, and I enjoyed every moment of the excitement created by the crowd of around 60,000. But what struck me most about the games was that I do not believe Jamaica was expecting much of a big performance outside of the sprints. But once we started the competition, I trailed only for the first two events after poor performances in the 100 meters and the long jump. After that first day I recovered and built a 270-point lead over my nearest competitor. It was the first time in a long time I had been able to relax on the second day of the decathlon and enjoy the moment. What I did not realize was that I was making history. I was to become the first athlete from an English-speaking Caribbean island to win the event. That made the victory much more special. There I was, a boy from Burnt Savannah and St. Elizabeth making history in one of the greatest sporting events on the planet. Of the four gold medals Jamaica won at the games, the one for the decathlon belonged to me.

I collected my gold medal and watched as the Jamaican flag was slowly raised to the strains of the island's national anthem. I realized that only a select few ever experience a moment like that, hearing your country's national anthem being played in your honor. That is a once-in-a-lifetime dream. But there was also something almost mystical going on inside me, the same feeling I had felt when I had won the NCAA title earlier that year. I felt a yearning that no win could fill. In fact, I felt the people in the stadium were more elated for my triumph than I was. "What is that feeling of emptiness I am experiencing? This should be the happiest moment of my life." I buried the feeling and saluted the crowd as the Jamaican national anthem faded into the breeze.

As 2002 drew to a close I competed in my first pro meet in late September, finishing eighth in Talence, France. It had been a long but successful season. I was then selected as a finalist for Jamaica's Sportsman of the Year award. I finished second runner-up, a position I was honored to receive. I also was named Jamaica's International Collegiate Athlete of the Year and was ranked among the top ten decathletes in the world. All that recognition led to a modest shoe contract. In addition, I had opened the door for other talented Jamaican athletes. Who would follow?

My focus turned to qualifying for the 2004 Olympic Games in Athens, Greece. But before I could head there, there were some stops to make along the way. As 2003 started I finished eighth in the famous Hypo-Meeting in Gotzis, Austria, and then finished ninth in Paris at the World Championships, which also marked the emergence of fellow Jamaican Usain Bolt on the world stage.

I won my first decathlon as a pro in Desenzano, Italy, in 2004. I followed that with a twelfth-place finish at the Hypo-Meeting back in Gotzis a few weeks later. Then it was time to focus on a strong performance in the upcoming Olympic Games in Athens where Jamaica would be represented by not one but two decathletes.

The years that led to those 2004 Olympic Games had been a challenge financially. Even though I had signed a modest contract with a shoe company, the proceeds were not enough to sustain proper training. I believed being Jamaican was why my contract was not better. Most shoe companies did not recognize Jamaican athletes much outside of sprinting. It did not matter to them how good I was or how much potential and promise I was showing, but not having proper support puts an athlete at a disadvantage. As a result, my focus had to shift from properly preparing for the Olympic Games to making money to support my endeavor.

That meant I competed as much as I could to win money so I could properly train. But all that competition came at a price. Too much competition results in not enough time for fundamental training, and that limits an athlete's long-term progress toward a successful career and realization of his true potential. I reached out to many Jamaican companies for financial support, but with no luck. Jamaica lacked a strong support system at the time for an athlete like myself, so I had to reach out to Olympic Solidarity, an organization that helps support athletes for two years before the Olympic Games.

* * *

One minute before my last run I heard the soft voice of Coach Boo as my teammate Walter Davis and I lined up to run the 150 meters that would complete our Saturday morning workout of 1x300 meters, 2x250 meters, 2x200 meters, and 3x150 meters. I could feel my body aching, but we both yearned for an Olympic medal. It was about a week before I would leave for Jamaica's Olympic training camp in Nuremberg, Germany. Stuff inside me that I didn't know I had helped me push through in 16.8 seconds. Walter and I both fell to the ground, bodies aching, but I knew I was ready.

Walter Davis was a USA national champion in both the horizontal jumps and a four-time World Championship medalist in the triple jump. Walter was the first US Olympian from Barton (County) Community College in Great Bend, Kansas. Walter's versatility helped him qualify for the 2000 US Olympic roster in both the triple jump and the long jump at the age of twenty-one, but he chose to compete in only the triple jump in Sydney. He was part of my LSU men's team that had won the 2002 NCAA outdoor crown, and he had won both the long jump (26' 6¼") and the triple jump (56' 10¾"). Then he combined with Pete Coley, Benny Brazell, and Robert Parham to win the 4x100-meter relay in 38.32 seconds. Also in 2002, Davis posted five of the top six triple jumps by Americans. He was a reliable training partner with both speed and stamina. I knew I was ready when I saw Walter on the ground rolling over for the first time in the four years we had been training together.

Pre-Olympic Games 2004 Training Camp

Nuremberg is located in the German state of Bavaria and has a population of about

500,000. It was considered the center of the German Renaissance in the fifteenth and sixteenth centuries and, in 1525, Nuremberg accepted the Protestant Reformation that brought the religious Peace of Nuremberg in 1532 when the Lutherans gained important concessions. Nuremberg also was considered the unofficial capital of the Holy Roman Empire.

In modern times, the Nazi Party used the city to hold its rallies in the late 1920s and most of the 1930s. But what left an impression on me—and the world—was what transpired after the end of World War II in 1945-46.

The city was the site of the infamous Nuremberg Trials that saw the Allies try thirteen cases against many leading Nazis who were charged with war crimes against Jews in particular and humanity in general. To establish a strong case against the Nazis who had claimed they were merely following orders, the Allied Tribunal held that the creation laws held a higher standard than any laws created by men. In other words, the Allies relied on God to win the day in court.

* * *

The seven-day pre-Olympic training camp in Nuremberg was a success. I worked on fine-tuning for the games in Athens and was thrilled to have another talented Jamaican, Maurice Smith, a product of Calabar High School and Auburn University in Alabama, join me in preparing for the decathlon. Athens would be the first time Jamaica would be represented by two decathletes at any level. That was the dream I had longed for—to open the door for another multitalented Jamaican athlete to step through. Maurice did.

As the plane left Nuremberg for Greece and the birthplace of the Olympic Games, my thoughts were on getting down to business.

Olympic Games 2004 – Athens, Greece

We landed in Athens and were immediately taken to the athlete's village to be accredited and issued our credentials. I was in dreamland once again. There I was, about to compete in the largest athletic event the planet had to offer in the ancient city of Athens, the cradle of Western civilization.

Once we settled into the athlete's village we played dominoes, watched movies, and just hung-out with each other and told jokes to pass the time. The much-awaited Opening Ceremony was scheduled for August 13 in the main Olympic stadium. Fireworks lit the night skies, drums played, and planes flew over the stadium. The Opening Ceremony was a beautiful portrayal of Greek mythology that traced the path from the ancient Games to the modern Games. Stories of Greek mythology were enacted, including one that featured a centaur.

The 2004 Olympic Games was a splendid artistic display of Greek arts and culture. Following that wonderful display the nations participating in the Games were paraded for the world to see, after which the lighting of the Olympic torch signaled the Games had officially begun. The crowd roared in appreciation as the torch was lit and the announcer declared, "Let the Games begin!"

August 23, 2004 – Day One of the Decathlon

Ten days after the start of the Games, thirty-nine athletes were ready to compete in the decathlon. As we entered the Olympic stadium through the tunnel we were met with great anticipation from the half-full stadium. As we were introduced, I was wearing my yellow vest with green tights and sunglasses. I waved to the crowd and was loudly applauded. That was another dream come true.

The decathlon was to begin with the 100 meters at 9:15 a.m. I was in the first heat, which included the current world record holder Roman Sebrle from the Czech Republic. He was favored to win the decathlon in Athens, and he was an athlete I admired. As we walked from the warm-up area to the track, I could feel myself bursting with excitement. "This is it—the long-awaited moment," I thought, "a moment to make my mark." I was ready.

"On your marks!" The stadium fell silent as the starter raised his gun to the skies. "Set!" I waited. I could see the finish line, and my goal was to get there fast and first. When the gun went off I reacted quickly, head down, driving out of the blocks. At about 30 meters I took control of the race and scampered to the finish line to the applause of the crowd, winning with a time of 10.69, fast for a decathlete. That turned out to be the sixth fastest time of all the heats, and I moved within fifty points of the event leader, Bryan Clay of the USA. That was a good start for me, and I was ready for the next event, the long jump.

Hands raised high into the air, I beckoned the fans to clap as I prepared for my first attempt. I could feel the rhythm of the crowd as I started my approach, gradually increasing my speed as I hurtled down the runway. I hit the board at maximum speed, and I knew it was a good jump. As I landed I could see the 8-meter mark a little behind me. I then turned to see the judge's white flag. I was excited and acknowledged the crowd. I knew that jump could dramatically change the competition in my favor. I waited for the mark to be posted; finally, the board read 7.48 meters. That could not be . . . my jump was much farther than that. What could have gone wrong? Did some part of my body touch the sand pit before I landed? No, the replay did not show any part of my body touching the pit early. But by the time I could protest, the pit had already been raked clean.

I was devastated; a dream start that could have given me great momentum going into the shot put and, possibly, an opportunity to move into second after two events had been snuffed out like a puff of sand on a windy day. What could I do?

Any true decathlete must learn to push through the competition and forget what was behind and focus only on what was ahead, so I tried to move on. But instead of having one of the best long jump marks of the competition, I finished eighth. Moving on was tough because momentum plays such a key role in the decathlon. My disappointment carried over to the shot put, at least somewhat. The shot put usually was a strong event for me, but not that time. I ended up throwing a modest 14.80 meters, well below my best and only good enough for fourteenth overall.

Next was the high jump. Athletes were required to have thirty-five minutes rest after the completion of each event before beginning the next one, so I took my markers and sat down to wait for the event to start. The high jump was another event that was usually strong for me. But by the time I had taken my first jump, more than half the field had already completed the event and were resting and preparing for the next event, the 400 meters.

On my first attempt at 2.15 meters (7' 1/4"), I noticed a group of officials hanging around the pit area. I finished with three near misses, much to the agony of the crowd and me. As soon as I emerged from the pit after my last jump I was told I had to head to the 400-meter start line immediately as I was in the first heat. I protested and said I needed time to recover, and I asked to be moved to the last heat, which would have allowed me ample time to see my massage therapist and properly prepare for the race. I pointed out that most of the athletes had enjoyed well over an hour rest, and I should be allowed at least the mandated thirty-five minutes. The official's next statement came as a shocker: I was told if I did not run in the first heat I would be disqualified from the rest of the decathlon. The reason I was given was that they had to honor TV's commercial time slot.

That was heart-wrenching. I had moved into fifth place and was in a prime position to challenge for a medal. But the Games were not about the athletes anymore; they were about money. I felt cheap. I felt as used as a beat-up doormat. How could the Olympics fall so low? A once-in-a-lifetime dream for most athletes was being compromised to pay the bills, but without the athletes there would be no commercial opportunities and no modern Olympic Games. To this day, I would still like to know who was responsible for making that crucial and unfair decision.

As I walked to the 400-meter starting line, my mind was whirling, and my veins were filled with rage. Then I thought back to my childhood when I had seen the planes flying overhead and wondered where they were going. I had wanted to be on a plane traveling to an unknown destination for an adventure. And there I was, on the biggest stage of my life, in the midst of a great adventure, only to be cheated. But I guess that is part of the intrigue of adventuring; things don't always go as you imagined they would. Finally, I said to myself, "I am going to give this race my best shot." I approached the starting line and took a few light turns on the curve in an effort to save my legs but not enough to get into a rhythm. Then I waited for the starter's gun.

"On your marks!" All I remember after that was the gun sounding. I took off like a man on a mission and shot up the track. As I entered the final curve toward the finish line I was ahead of the field. I could feel my legs tiring, but I pressed on and told myself, "No matter what, I am going to win this race." And I did, but I was still upset at the end, for I knew I had much more in the tank.

At the end of the first day I was in sixth position with 4,408 points, a shockingly good score to some, but a far cry from where I wanted to be. As I cooled down at the warm-up track late into the Greek night I stepped into the bucket of ice water prepared for the athletes to help numb the pain and reduce the soreness of the long day of events. I could not help reflecting on what could have been had I been treated fairly in the long jump and before the 400 meters.

As I said before, the decathlon is so much about momentum, and when you are in a strong position, it's easier to relax and compete within yourself while your competitors are forced to try harder and, possibly, make more mistakes in trying to catch you. With the second day on the horizon, I would have to give it everything I had left to challenge for a medal.

My freezing body reminded me it was time to get out of the ice bucket and head back to the athlete's village to get some rest. By the time we returned it was after one in the morning. I grabbed a quick bite in the cafeteria and went to my sleeping quarters. I would have to be up before 6 a.m., only a few hours away, to begin the second day of the decathlon.

August 24, 2004 – Day Two of the Decathlon

About 5:30 a.m. I rolled out of bed with a sore body that ached all over. I ran to the bathroom and took a cold shower to get rid of the soreness and the groggy feeling. I then set off to the cafeteria to grab a bite before heading to the stadium for the 9 a.m. start of the 110-meter hurdles.

It was a bright sunny morning as we entered the stadium through the warm-up tunnel. I was excited. I needed a good start in the hurdles to climb higher in the standings, and that was an opportunity I was relishing. The hurdles had become a good event for me.

As we settled into our blocks I had one goal: run like I had never run before in the decathlon hurdles. As the starter raised his gun and fired, I bolted out and attacked the first hurdle. It was a dream start, a far cry from my first hurdle race. I was running like a pro and won with my second fastest hurdle time ever, 14.17 seconds. I was on a high afterward. That was the perfect start I had been hoping for, and it moved me into fifth place. I was in a great position going into one of my favorite events, the discus. But the discus did not go as planned. With the pressure mounting to produce a big throw, I barely reached 44.75 meters. I had allowed the pressure to get to me, and instead of focusing on the event at hand, I started looking ahead. That is a fatal mistake for almost any athlete in almost any sport at almost any level, and the Olympic decathlon certainly was no exception.

After the letdown from the discus I nearly missed the opening height in the pole vault, but I managed to finish with a jump of 4.40 meters, good for a guy with a personal best of 4.50 meters, but the mistake in the discus was having a domino effect. As I struggled through the javelin, I entered the final event, the 1500 meters, in sixth place.

My coach and I had devised a new strategy for the 1500 meters. We had been working on me running from the back instead of leading and then holding on, although I loved to do that. In front of a packed house, the race started with the new plan working perfectly. I was to start my final kick to the finish with 600 meters to go, but when I reached the 600-meter mark a moment of doubt crossed my mind. Would I be able to bring it home as strongly as we had planned?

I decided to wait until the last 400 meters, at the sound of the final lap bell, to make my move. But by the time I reached the last 200 meters I realized I still had plenty left in the tank. I finished with a good time of 4:36.31, but I was upset with myself. That split-second doubt ended up costing me as I dropped to ninth with 8,225 points, only fifty points from sixth. That was still a national record for Jamaica and a personal best for me, but it was a bittersweet moment. It was hard not to think about what could have been had a few calls gone my way, and if I had executed a few events better on that second day.

I could feel the tears in my eyes. I knew those opportunities are once in a lifetime for most people, and that had been mine. Even so, as the athletes assembled in the stadium and waved goodbye to the cheering crowd, I knew Maurice Smith and I had done Jamaica proud. Maurice had turned in a wonderful performance to finish in fourteenth place. We had put Jamaica on the decathlon map, and I had seen my dream realized: someone else had taken up the challenge, and I had been there to witness it. It would be Maurice's turn to take the event further.

Afterward, while I was cooling down, Coach Boo told me how proud he was of my performance. I was one of the top ten athletes in the world. I had come a long way from the rocky playgrounds of Burnt

Savannah, St. Elizabeth, to Athens where the greatest athletic event of all had begun. I smiled to myself and took a dip in the ice buckets; then it was finally time to see Athens for myself.

Chapter Eight

The Picture Becomes Clearer

As I climbed the hills overlooking the ancient city of Athens toward the famous Acropolis (which means "the highest point" in Greek) and the ancient buildings of great historical and architectural significance, my eyes focused on the famous 3,000-year-old structure of the Parthenon, a temple constructed to honor the Greek goddess Athena. The Parthenon is regarded as an enduring symbol of Ancient Greece, Athenian democracy, and Western civilization. It is one of the world's greatest cultural monuments.

The Parthenon was converted into a church honoring the Virgin Mary in the latter part of the sixth century and later was converted to a mosque after the Ottoman Empire's conquest.

Now high above the Greek skies, the ruins of that structure, once worshipped and admired for its magnificence, is still majestic, yet it is only a shadow of its original self. That building rose out of man's desire for conquest and dominion. And there on the Acropolis, a thought hit me: Look around, look at all this splendor, but what will it mean a couple of hundred years from now? My mind raced back to the wonderful Olympic Games I had just participated in, a competition that had paraded the world's finest athletes with as much splendor as the ancient Romans had presented the gladiators, but where were they now? They were mere footnotes in history.

The hills of the Acropolis also brought me back to my childhood years when I would climb the hills in front of my home and look back in awe at the shared beauty of Burnt Savannah that extended all the way to the swamp. I could see all over Athens from where I was perched. How many people had been amazed by that wondrous sight? I came from a beautiful place with beautiful scenery. And there I was in another place on another hill soaking up another beautiful scene.

History tells us that Athens featured fine arts, politics, religion and, of course, athletics, and it was the pinnacle of Western civilization, but what happened to the people who constructed that culture? Were they happy and fulfilled?

On the hills of the Acropolis I came to realize that the feeling I experienced when I climbed those hills in Burnt Savannah was a feeling no athletic competition could give me. It was as if creation had come alive and said, "Feel me, breathe me, touch me, and be at peace." In the athletic competition that I kept pursuing, and pursuing, and pursuing I never attained such fulfillment, not even on top of the podiums of victory. There was always that missing feeling. I started to realize that the doors that had opened for me were not simply for the purpose of exploiting my athletic talents; they were to help me experience greater fulfillment as a human being.

I have come to realize that, even in the darkest places in this world, there is always a light. That light lit my pathway even when I did bad things. That light helped me emerge from the discouragement I encountered throughout my young life. I can look back today and say to the people of Burnt Savannah, I love you for what I experienced because discouragement gave me the stamina to strive for higher and loftier goals. I do not know what would have become of my life had my path been easier. And hear me: I am not saying that I would not have been a successful athlete had I not encountered those negativities. I am saying I learned to persevere through any difficulty. And by the time I started high school at Munro College, even though I faced intense discouragement, especially from some people I thought to be my friends, I was able to shrug it off and stay focused on my goals. There was a plan for my life to take me elsewhere, for me to be a leader. But why me? That I cannot answer . . . not yet.

On the hills of Munro College, as the school motto says, "In Acre Sitam Quis Occultabit" (a city on a hill cannot be hidden), I found a purpose and the resources to pursue my goals. On those same hills I became a man, an athlete, and a Jamaican icon. On the hill of the Acropolis I started realizing that on the hills of my life I had found myself and my purpose. On those hills of life I had found the truth, and the most important truth I had found was over 2,000 years old. That truth came from a hill far from Burnt Savannah, St. Elizabeth. On that hill one whose hands were stretched out was lifted up so I could find peace. For just like in the 2004 Athens Olympic Games, there were always the questions afterward: Had I done my best? Had some things gone differently in the competition or if some other decisions had been made, would I have earned my medal? Then the thought came back to me: I had been on top of many podiums, but still I was not fulfilled.

Even though I grew up between two churches and was exposed to great teachings, it took me traveling the world and experiencing athletic glory to fully understand who or what was guiding my life. You may ask what all that means. It means that even though you might be in a place saturated with water, you can still go thirsty. I had a thirst, a thirst for purpose and meaning. I had deep questions and longings from my earliest childhood.

That does not mean we cannot find our true purpose where we are. It only means my path was different. There were always things that appealed to me in my place of birth, but they did not provide the answers I sought. I was always seeking, and I now realize that the Great Power who guides this universe can find you wherever you are and use you to accomplish great things. Track and field was my vehicle.

As I came to find out in Nuremberg, even in one of the darkest periods in human history at the end of World War II when the world was in great conflict and great pain, mankind's laws were not the basis that brought justice to those who carried out some of the greatest atrocities in history. Instead, an appeal to the Highest Power convicted those Nazi war criminals.

On the Acropolis hill in Athens I also saw that humanity, in its zeal to accomplish great things built the Parthenon, but even that great civilization could not stop the reality that such a magnificent structure would one day lie in ruins.

When all the dots are connected, from Mr. Walker to LW, to Gwyn, to Leroy Allison, and beyond, I realized that the ultimate truth is not what this world has to offer but what lies beyond, a truth without question.

The hand of time has painted this beautiful story of my life. He is the great author, the master painter, for only the artist knows where to place all the strokes and how to connect all the dots to create such a picture. We must remember that walking in

God's will is not the same as trying to create our own destiny. I have come to believe that anything done outside the will of God will have no lasting effect, so surrender your will to Him and you, too, can move mountains.

Burnt Savannah Primary School

Munro College High School

Louisiana State University (LSU)

Commonwealth Games 2002, gold medal

The Parthenon, Athens, Greece, after 2004 Olympic Games

Long jump, Athens, Greece, Olympics

Getting ready for the javelin throw in Athens, Greece, Olympics

110-meter hurdles, Manchester, England, Commonwealth Games

The end of the race and the beginning of retirement.

About the Author: Claston Anthony Bernard

Claston A. Bernard was born in 1979 in the district of Burnt Savannah, St. Elizabeth, Southwest Jamaica. A 1998 graduate of Munro College High School, he went on to Louisiana State University on a track scholarship and earned a degree in Human Resource Management in May 2002.

Bernard later became the first Commonwealth Games gold medalist for Jamaica or any English-speaking Caribbean country. The first decathlete to ever represent Jamaica in the Olympic Games, Bernard is a two-time Jamaica Olympian, finishing ninth in the 2004 Games in Athens after participating in the 2000 Games in Sydney. He also is an NCAA champion and a four-time SEC champion.

Printed by Libri Plureos GmbH in Hamburg, Germany